Embroidery on Paper for Every Occasion

Joke and Adriaan de Vette

Cantecleer

Content

Foreword	3	Early Bloomers	42
General Techniques	4	New Life	46
The Great Outdoors	10	Children's Birthday	50
Animals	14	Sports All Year Round	54
A Moment Alone	18	A Lovely Summer Day	58
Birds	22	A Day Outdoors	62
Sympathy Cards	26	Autumn is Upon us Once Again	66
Good Wishes	30	Autumn Comfort	70
Christmas Cards	34	Lovely Christmas and New Year's Greetings	73
Whimsical Animals	38		

First published in the Netherlands by Tirion Publishers in 1999 and in 2000 as
Er op uit met borduren op papier and Borduren op papier het hele jaar door

© 2004 Tirion Uitgevers bv, Baarn

Reprinted in 2006

ISBN 90 213 3517 4

Translation: Cindi Michele Beckman, Studio Imago
DTP: Studio Imago, Amersfoort
Photography: Hennie Raaymakers, St. Michielsgestel
Photography styling: Willemien Mommersteeg, St. Michielsgestel
Illustrator: Sjaak van Went

This book is published by
Uitgeverij Cantecleer
Postbus 309
3740 AH Baarn
The Netherlands

Cantecleer is an imprint of Tirion Publishers bv

Many thanks for the great ideas and support in different ways to: my husband Adriaan, Sjaak van Went, Marga de Jonge, Ria Winckers, Riet Groen in 't Woud, Annemarie Paalvast en Cathia Roth.
Grateful acknowledgement is also made to Kars, Papicolor, Omnium and Romak for the supplied materials.

Foreword

It is with great pleasure that I created the 69 embroidery patterns for the "Every Occasion" theme that is the basis of this book. The cards shown in this book pertain to the four seasons and seasonal occasions.

There are a number of round and square cards shown in the book, but all patterns can be embroidered onto standard rectangular cards. The cards give you a variety of ideas for using coloured paper and thread, a serration tool, patterned scissors, corner scissors, or a photo corner punch. Do not feel obligated to create the cards exactly as shown in the book. Add your own touches and decorations. You can also add additional small embroidery patterns along the edges and corner patterns.

This book offers you even more variations as well as a new option. If you find the embroidery to be too difficult or time-consuming, you can simply punch out the pattern on the card and colour it in using different coloured gel pens. Simply trace the lines from hole to hole. Metallic pens produce particularly attractive effects. And the result resembles embroidery. Aafke Boorsma invented this technique after losing the ability to embroider due to a disability. After viewing her work, I was so impressed by the results that I highly recommend trying out this technique. It's a whole new way to embroider!

You can also visit my website:
www.geocities.com/adrvette

I wish you much enjoyment and success in your creative endeavours.

Joke
de Vette

General Techniques

Pattern

Using a copier, copy the patterns from the book. Use paperclips to attach the cutout pattern to the card. You can also use cellotape, but this often leaves adhesive glue behind on the card that can later smudge. The patterns for many of the cards consist of two parts: the main pattern that must be perforated in the middle of the card and a pattern for the edge or corners of the card. There is a frame around the main pattern to help you centre the pattern on the card. Most frames are narrower than the card, however. It is therefore advisable to cut out the patterns so that they are the same width as the card. This will enable you to centre the pattern properly.

Piercing

Place a sheet of decorative rubber on the piercing cushion and then place the card with pattern (to be pierced) on top of that. The rubber will make the perforated holes more attractive. Use a fine piercing pen for piercing and hold it upright when piercing. Try to pierce the holes as carefully as possible for a more polished finish. Do not make the holes too large because you will need to turn the card over repeatedly when embroidering in order to see what you are doing and, if the holes are too large, the needle will keep falling out of the card.

Embroidering

The embroidery threads used in this book are from Sulky unless stated otherwise. The colour numbers for the thread and the embroidery stitches used are given for every card. Tape the ends of each thread to the back of the card using cellotape.

Finishing

The perforated holes may still be visible after you have finished embroidering. To make them less noticeable, rub the back of the card with a smooth round object after embroidering to rub the holes closed. A teaspoon works well. The insert sheet is used to cover the back of the embroidery work (glue the insert sheet to the card only on the left side, see drawing).

Embroidery stitches

The descriptions of the stitches given here may be different than what you are used to. I have described a number of different stitches here in order to enable you to embroider the cards more easily and without using charts. Many stitches are similar to one another even though they have different names; only their shape is different because the perforated holes take on a different shape. The basic stitch formation is shown in bold. The repetitions are drawn with thinner lines.

Embroidery Materials Required

- Piercing cushion
- Sheet of decorative rubber
- Fine piercing tool (Pergamano one-needle perforating pen)
- Fine embroidery needles
- Embroidery/sewing machine threads (such as ◆ Sulky metallic)
- Cellotape
- 180 to 270 gram paper
- Insert sheets: 120 gram white paper
- Paperclips
- Waterless glue, such as photo glue or UHU magic stick
- Copy of the perforation patterns
- Gel or ballpoint pens
- 0.3 mm propelling pencil or HB pencil with sharp point
- Rubber
- Optional: cutting mat, utility knife with retractable blade, ruler, decorative edge scissors and punches

Running stitch (not shown)

A running stitch is one stitch that goes from point A to point B.

Backstitch

The backstitch is only used to embroider very small lines or curves, such as a small eye.

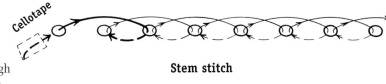

Backstitch

First, insert the needle through the first hole of the line from the back to the front and then through the second hole from the front to the back. Repeat continuously. To create a closed line, the stitch first runs forward and then back. See drawing.

Stem stitch

The stem stitch is used for larger details and to create thicker lines. Insert the needle through the first hole of the line

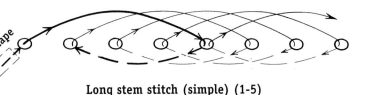

Stem stitch

from the back to the front. Skip a hole on the front of the card and go back one hole on the back. This is the basis of the stem stitch. Keep repeating the stitch.

Long stem stitch (simple)

The long stem stitch produces a cordlike embroidered line.

There are two ways to do a long stem stitch.

Long stem stitch (simple) (1-5)

The easiest way is to use the same method as the standard stem stitch, but you make longer stitches. For example, skip three holes on the front (1-5) and then go back three holes on the back. See drawing.

This stitch can be made even longer. For example, skip seven holes on the front and go back seven holes on the back. A drawback to this embroidery technique is that you end up using a lot of thread on the back of the card.

Tip
Don't count the holes when doing a long stem stitch (simple)! Guess the number of holes that you go back on the back.

Shortening or lengthening the long stem stitch

If you are approaching a short curve or want a thinner line, shorten the long stem stitch. Make the return stitch a little shorter and go back to the first empty hole with the forward stitch. Continue with the new stitch length. If you have passed a curve or want a thicker line, lengthen the long stem stitch. Make the return stitch a little longer, etc. This can be used for both the simple version as well as for the standard long stem stitch.

Tip
Don't think about it too much! Lengthen or shorten the stitch, don't worry about precision. This way you'll learn it quickly and you'll feel confident enough to use it.

Long stem stitch (standard)

Long stem stitch (standard) (1-5)

This version produces the same cordlike line as the simple version but requires less thread. As shown in the drawing, you go back and forth on the front of the card using long stitches of equal length. On the back you go to the next hole. Do the basic stitch shown in bold and continue repeating it.

You can also make the stitch shorter or longer than is shown in the drawing. The forward stitches on the back of the card help you maintain a constant stitch length. With a stitch length of 1-5 or 1-7 or 1-9 (and so on), the backstitches on the back of the card form a closed line.

Circle stitch

The circle stitch is the same as the long stem stitch (standard), but is easier to do because it's easier to see what you are doing. This can be clearly seen from the drawing.

Circle stitch (1-5)

Embroider back and forth on the front of the card using long stitches of equal length. Do a small stitch on the back to the next hole. The stitches on the back therefore always go in the same direction. Draw an arrow on the back to avoid mistakes.

Start with any hole, count the right number of holes, and insert through the front. Complete the basic stitch shown in bold without counting. Repeat the basic stitch until the circle is complete. There should be two threads in every hole.

Embroidering curves

The circle stitch can also be used to embroider curves and arches. When finished, the start and end of the line will be slightly thin. Simply add another one or two stitches, as shown in bold in the drawing.

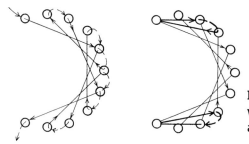

Embroidered curve with extra stitches at the ends

Filling stitch

The filling stitch is a variation on the circle stitch. It is used to fill in shapes like circles and stars.

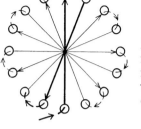

Filling stitch: There must be an equal number of holes to the right and left of the first stitch

The first stitch runs from the front through the middle to the opposite side of the figure. There must be an equal number of holes on the left and right of the first stitch or it will not work properly.

Complete the basic stitch shown in bold in the drawing and repeat until the figure is filled. All stitches on the back run in the same rotational direction. Draw an arrow on the back to avoid mistakes.

Filler stitch

The filler stitch fills up part of the space between two lines, whether or not they meet at the ends. The stitches are not always of equal length, but otherwise the embroidering technique is the same as with the circle stitch. Only after all crisscrossing lines have been embroidered do we stitch a thread across the rows of holes.

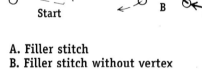

A. Filler stitch
B. Filler stitch without vertex

Fan stitch

The fan stitch is used for embroidering solid petals and similar shapes. It can also be used to fill a circle. The centre hole from which all stitches originate must be made larger than the other holes.

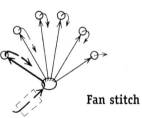

Fan stitch

Stitch from back to front through the centre hole. At the edge of the figure, stitch through the front to the back again, and then again through the centre hole through the back to the front. This is the basis of the fan stitch. Repeat this stitch until the entire figure is filled. Try to avoid crossing the threads.

Loop stitch

The loop stitch resembles the fan stitch, but is more suitable for larger petals and fans that require a lot of thread. It is almost impossible for the threads of the loop stitch to cross each other, thereby creating a more attractive effect. There is also less thread on the back.

Start by making a loop (see drawings A and B). Insert from the back to the front through hole 1 and then from the front to the back through hole 2. Repeat this one more time. The result is a strong double loop. Now insert from the back to the front for the third time through hole 1 and go to the middle hole on the edge of the figure. Place a piece of cellotape over the loop on the back of the card to strengthen the thread. Go one hole to the left or right on the back.

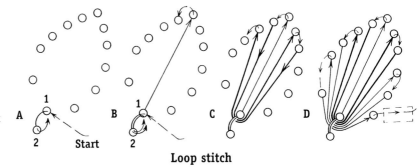

Loop stitch

The basic stitches are shown in bold in drawing C. Only insert to the back of the card along the edge of the figure. You stay on the front of the card at the loop. Place your needle almost flat against the paper and stitch under the loop. Now stitch in the other direction under the loop. Repeat the basic stitches until the figure is filled (see drawing D).

Zigzag stitch

The zigzag stitch may feel odd to do at first because you are not moving forward on the front of the card but rather backward at a slight diagonal. The forward stitches are done on the back.

Do the zigzag stitch between two lines with more or less the same number of holes. This stitch can be used for any shape.

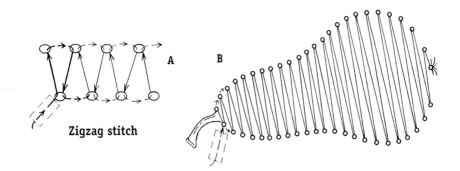

Zigzag stitch

Two stitches are shown in bold in drawing A. These stitches are the basis of the zigzag stitch. Continue repeating these stitches until the entire figure is filled.

Important! To start properly, you will need to make sure the first stitch is also running backward at an angle. Make sure you start in the right hole (see drawing A).

Cross stitch

There are at least three good ways to embroider a cross stitch. The technique shown here is the same one used for the plait stitch. Each cross stitch must be completed before moving on to the next stitch.

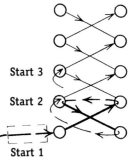

One of the ways to embroider the cross stitch

Plait stitch

The plait stitch is used to attractively fill in the space between two lines. The space could be wide, such as a candle, or narrow, such as the stem of a flower. Once you have gained experience, you will be able to use the plait stitch for any kind of shape.

There must be virtually the same number of holes on both lines. The basis of the plait stitch is simple because it is a cross stitch.

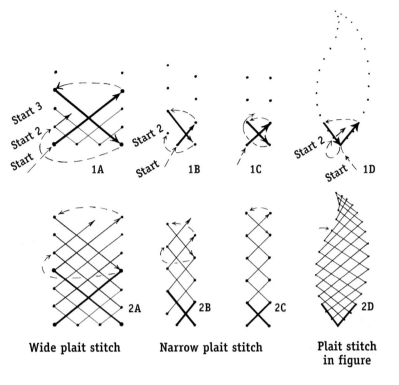

Wide plait stitch   **Narrow plait stitch**   **Plait stitch in figure**

Drawings 1A, 1B and 1C show the basic stitch in bold. Do this stitch and repeat it from the points marked 'start 2', 'start 3', and so on, until the figure is filled (see drawings 2A, 2B and 2C).

Once you've done a few stitches you'll be able to embroider further by feel. Most people are able to learn rather quickly.

A note on the wide plait stitch. In drawing 1A, there are a number of additional stitches shown as thin lines under the basic stitch. These determine the angle of the basic stitches. It is therefore advisable to start with these additional stitches and then do the basic stitches afterwards.

Using the plait stitch for figures

If the figure starts with a point, start with half of the cross stitch (see drawing 1D), followed by one or more lopsided cross stitches. Fill in the rest of the figure as shown in drawing 2D. To obtain a nice distribution of threads, you may need to 'improvise' a little (i.e. go to the next hole or skip one. See the arrow in drawing 2D).

The Great Outdoors

Spring and summer are perfect times of the year for spending time outdoors, taking a walk through the woods or bicycling. These cards are in excellent keeping with this theme. If you know someone who is fond of bicycling, you could create the card with the bicycle on it, and the card with the signpost could be used as an invitation for a leisurely stroll. And for those fond of more active sports, the windsurfer card is the perfect choice.

Signpost

Pierce pattern 1A (see page 77) into the card (see General Techniques on page 4). Embroider the post in silver (7001) using the plait stitch. Embroider the signs using the long stem stitch 1-5. Stop when you get to the corners and start again. If the corner line is too thin, add a few stitches. The wavy sign pointing to the sea is embroidered in peacock blue (7052) using the standard stem stitch (1-3). The figures on the signs are all embroidered using the standard stem stitch. The lines behind the bicycle are embroidered using the backstitch. The colours shown here are pine green (7056) for the car and tent, gold (7007) for the bicycle, Xmas green (7018) for the shoe, dark copper (7010) for the castle with light copper (7011) for the door. The swimmer symbol is embroidered in dark copper (7010) and the water below it in peacock blue (7052). Embroider a blue (7016) line along the outline of the pole. It is easier to embroider this line after the rest is finished.

Carriage

This is not an easy card to make, but it is a fun challenge. Make sure you carry out the instructions in the order given below in order to avoid running into problems. See the General Techniques section on page 4 for the stitches used. Pierce pattern 1B into the card. The loop stitch is used five times for the hood. First embroider the four folds in the hood in lavender (7012). Every fold has its own loop (see drawing). Next, embroider the braces supporting the hood in rose (7013). All brace threads run under the first loop. The seat cushion for the coachman is embroidered using the plait stitch in rose (7013). The splashboard and the leaf spring next to the back wheel are embroidered in light copper (7011) using the long stem stitch 1-5. The rest is embroidered in dark gold (7004). The plait stitch is used for the armrest under the hood and for the drawbar. The long stem stitch 1-5 is used for the wagon part of the carriage. If

Tip
The cards in this chapter are embroidered on blue paper. If you choose a different coloured background, you may want to use different colour threads. You can also cut the cards out using patterned scissors and then glue them to a background. The insert sheet is then no longer necessary.

Pattern 1B

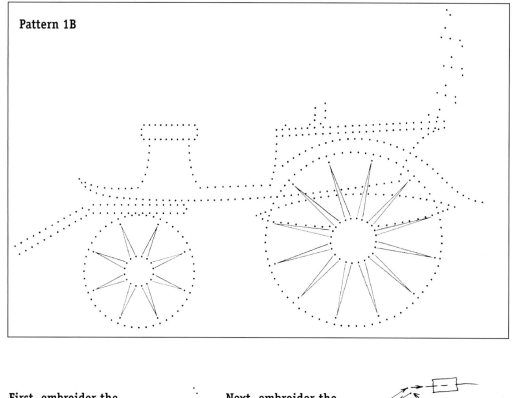

First, embroider the four folds in the hood using the loop stitch

Next, embroider the braces supporting the hood using the loop stitch

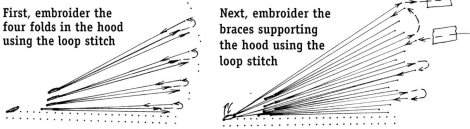

these lines end up too thin, you can always double them by embroidering them a second time using the same stitch. The wheels are embroidered last. Embroider the spokes first, as shown in the drawing. The hubs and rims should be done using the circle stitch: the hubs 1-5, the small wheel 1-7, and the large wheel 1-9.

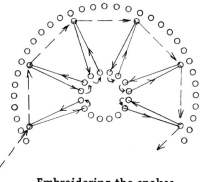

Embroidering the spokes

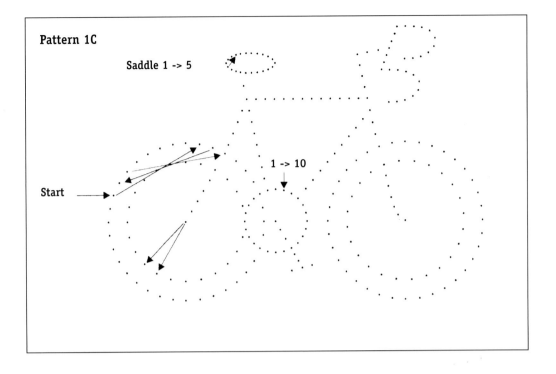

Pattern 1C

Saddle 1 -> 5

1 -> 10

Start

Bicycle

Pierce pattern 1C into the card (see General Techniques on page 4). The bicycle part of the card is embroidered entirely in variegated gold/turquoise/pink (7020). Start with the gear wheel with the pedals attached because now you can still see the perforated holes of the wheel clearly. Use the circle stitch 1-10. Next, embroider the frame, pedal, seat, and handlebars using the long stem stitch 1-5. Finally, embroider the spokes with running stitches and the tyres with the circle stitch 1-9.

Surfer

Pierce pattern 1D (page 77) into the card. For the stitches used, see General Techniques on page 5. Start by embroidering the mast using the plait stitch in variegated silver/rose/jade (7029). The boom that the surfer holds on to can also be embroidered with a plait stitch (with a little improvisation). If this is too difficult, use the long stem stitch 1-5 for the boom. Use the same colour as for the mast. For the board, use blue (7016) and embroider using the long stem stitch 1-5. Stop when you reach the point and start again. The sail should be embroidered in rose (7013) using the zigzag stitch and then using the long stem stitch 1-7. The two viewing panels in the sail should be embroidered using the standard stem stitch in Xmas green (7018). For the windsurfing suit, use peacock blue (7052) and embroider using the plait stitch and long stem stitch 1-5. The face, arms and legs should be done in lavender (7012) and using the long stem stitch 1-5. The waterline should be embroidered in silver (7001) and using the long stem stitch from 1 to 5. Once the card is finished, embroider the lines along the mast with the variegated threads.

Animals

Everyone loves animals. Many people, young and old, would enjoy receiving a lovely handmade animal card. You can use these cards for birthdays or to thank someone for a gift or enjoyable get-together. And it's lots of fun to create an animal card for someone. These cards are not too difficult to make and you can give them a nice added touch by cutting the edges with patterned scissors or decorating the corners with a punch. Use different coloured paper for the background and the result is a lovely card for any occasion.

Squirrels

Pierce pattern 3A into the card (see General Techniques on page 4). You can use the variegated threads or a soft golden colour for the squirrels. Embroider the entire card using the long stem stitch. To shorten or lengthen the long stem stitch, see General Techniques on page 5. For the top of the tail, start at the point and embroider using stitch length 1-9 and continue until the bottom of the back. For the underside of the tail, start again at the point, but this time using a stitch length of 1-5. Lengthen the stitches to 1-9 as soon as you complete the curve. This produces a smooth curve followed by a thicker line. Do the other lines in the following stitch lengths: 1-3 for hand and foot, 1-5 for head and front and hind legs, 1-5 for the nut (in a different colour).

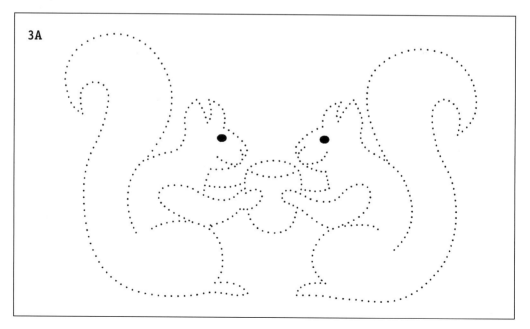

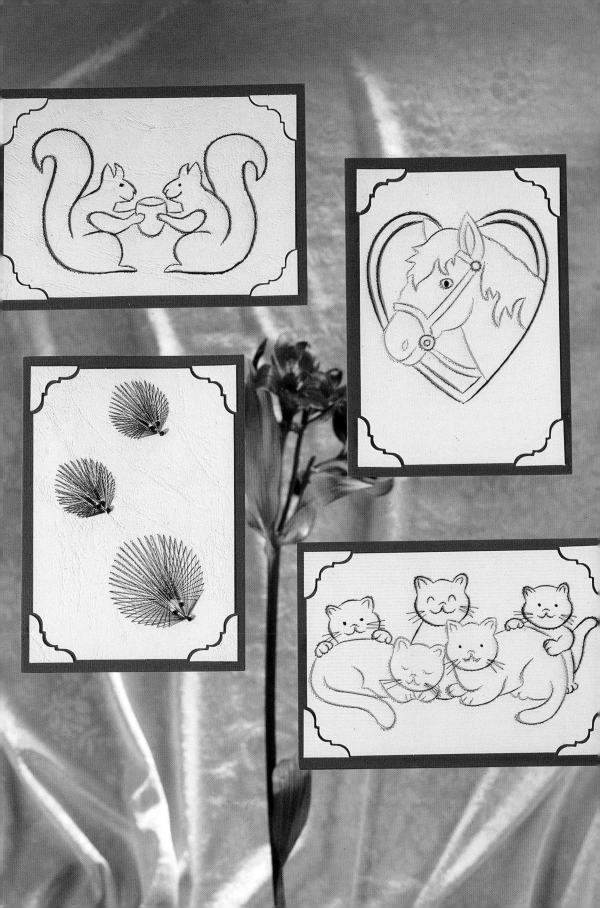

Hedgehogs

Choose pierce pattern 3B (see General Techniques on page 4). You obtain the spiny look of the hedgehogs by embroidering two layers on top of each other. The hedgehogs are done using the loop stitch. The following colours are used here: variegated gold/black (Madeira 252) for the bottom layer and gold (7007) for the upper layer. First make a double loop behind the eyes (see drawing). Make a long stitch from the back hole of the loop to the rearmost perforated hole of the hedgehog's body. Next, repeatedly stitch a V-shaped stitch under the loop. Use one hole to the left and one hole to the right of the first long thread. All holes left and right should be used. This is explained in detail on page 7

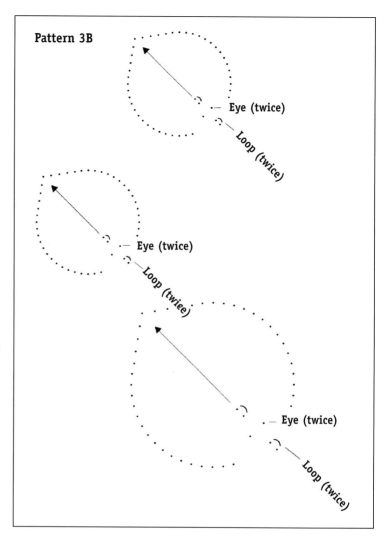

Pattern 3B

Eye (twice)

Loop (twice)

Eye (twice)

Loop (twice)

Eye (twice)

Loop (twice)

under General Techniques. The bottom layer is now complete and the upper layer can be embroidered. Make a double loop at the nose. Next, embroider the entire body the same way as the bottom layer. Finally, accentuate the nose with a small bead (use the two holes of the loop). Also use beads for the eyes.

Horse's Head

The use of bright colours will particularly appeal to children. The nobility of the horse is emphasised by the use of copper and gold and the darker coloured bridle. Pierce pattern 3C into the card (see General Techniques on page 4). The card is embroidered entirely using the stem stitch and the long stem stitch. The colours and stitches used here are as follows. Draw the eye in black. Embroider the heart in red (7054) using the long stem stitch 1-7. Do the eye and mane in light copper (7011), the rest of the head in gold (7007), the harness in mint (7053), and the rosettes in rainbow prism blue (7044). Embroider the short lines using the standard stem stitch and the longer lines using the long stem stitch 1-5. The eye and rosettes are embroidered from 1 to 4 (1-4).

Pattern 3D

The Cat Family

Pierce pattern 3D into the card (see General Techniques on page 4). Use whichever colours you desire. The following colours have been used here: gold (7007), dark copper (7010), light copper (7011) and black (7051). The cats are embroidered using the stem stitch and long stem stitch. The length of the stitches is up to you. Use short stitches for the short curves and short lines. Long lines can be made thicker by using a longer stitch. If a line appears too thin, simply embroider another line on top of it. Have fun!

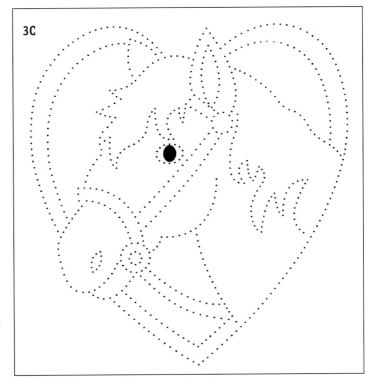

3C

A Moment Alone

These cards are about taking a moment for yourself, getting away from the hustle and bustle of life, enjoying the mementoes of your life and memories of loved ones in the privacy of your own home. Or spending time outdoors in the warmth of the sun and a summer breeze, the flowers, birds, clouds and sky all around, enjoying a moment of contemplation or day-dreaming. The images on these cards will be greatly appreciated by many.

Madonna and Child

Pierce pattern 5A (page 78) into the card (see General Techniques on page 4). This pattern is designed for A5 size paper. This Madonna and child card can also be framed with a mat. Embroider the veil in peacock blue (7052) and the cloak in blue (7016) using the long stem stitch 1-7. Embroider the face of the child, the Madonna and the hands in lavender (7012) using the standard stem stitch, and the child's arm using the long stem stitch 1-5. The details in the faces are embroidered in the same lavender colour using the backstitch or standard stem stitch. Embroider the child's robe in Xmas red (7014) using the long stem stitch 1-5. The child's hair should be done in light copper (7011) using the standard stem stitch. Embroider the halos in dark gold (7004) using the long stem stitch 1-7. Also do the S-shaped curls in gold using the long stem stitch 1-5. The stars between the curls should be in lavender. Embroider the outer border in red.

Book or Bible

Leave out the candle for those less interested in the bible. You then have a card with a book and a cup and saucer. Pierce pattern 5B (page 20) into the card. Pierce the holes for the text and for the bottom of the pages from left to right or the other way round. This will ensure a neat row of holes. It is important to pierce the holes precisely for this card, which is easy to embroider. Almost all instructions are clear from the pattern. Use the loop stitch for the candle flame and the plait stitch for the bottom of the candleholder. The embroidery stitches are explained under General Techniques on page 5. Embroider using a backstitch along the lower edge (the pages) as neatly as possible. The following colours are used here: red (7054) for the cover, gold (7007) for the pages and candle, variegated gold/black (Madeira 252) for the letters and candleholder and yellow (Madeira 1883) for the candle flame.

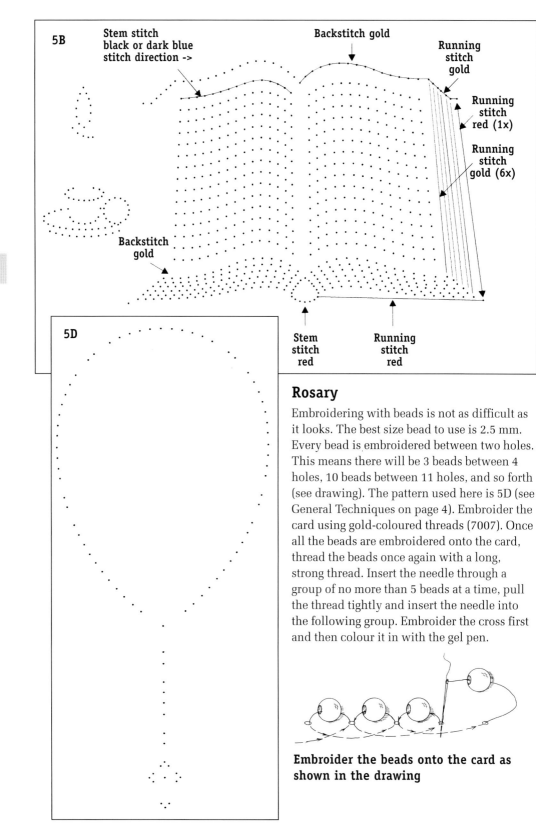

5B

Stem stitch
black or dark blue
stitch direction ->

Backstitch gold

Running
stitch
gold

Running
stitch
red (1x)

Running
stitch
gold (6x)

Backstitch
gold

5D

Stem
stitch
red

Running
stitch
red

Rosary

Embroidering with beads is not as difficult as
it looks. The best size bead to use is 2.5 mm.
Every bead is embroidered between two holes.
This means there will be 3 beads between 4
holes, 10 beads between 11 holes, and so forth
(see drawing). The pattern used here is 5D (see
General Techniques on page 4). Embroider the
card using gold-coloured threads (7007). Once
all the beads are embroidered onto the card,
thread the beads once again with a long,
strong thread. Insert the needle through a
group of no more than 5 beads at a time, pull
the thread tightly and insert the needle into
the following group. Embroider the cross first
and then colour it in with the gel pen.

**Embroider the beads onto the card as
shown in the drawing**

Pattern 5C

Candle

Additional materials for rosary

60 2.5 mm beads
Gold-coloured gel pen

Pierce pattern 5C into the card (see General Techniques on page 4). The colours used here are gold (7007) and jade green (7015). Embroider the card using the standard stem stitch for the short curves and the long stem stitch 1-5 or 1-7 for the longer lines. Embroider the candle using the running stitch and the flame using the loop stitch.

Birds

Birds are a part of everyday life. We hear and see them all day long. Whether sitting in the garden or on the balcony, we can see them fluttering about, looking for food. Some of the birds we see in the winter months are not at all shy and will even eat from a birdhouse or feeding balls hanging in the garden. City gardens are particularly popular with birds. Their singing starts before sunrise and, on lovely summer days, they give a coffee-time concert and provide the last sound of the day.

Bird on a Branch

Pierce pattern 7A into the card (see General Techniques on page 4). After piercing the pattern, colour in the eye. The pattern shows how the bird should be embroidered. Always start with the stitches that fill in the spaces and then embroider the outlines of those spaces afterwards.

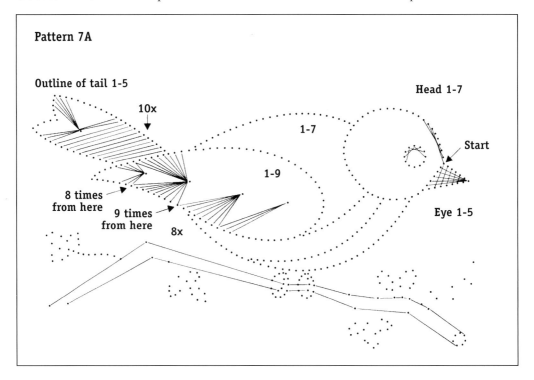

Pattern 7A

Outline of tail 1-5

Head 1-7

10x

1-7

Start

1-9

8 times from here

9 times from here

8x

Eye 1-5

The colours used here are Xmas red (7014), variegated cranberry/gold/pine green (7027), brass (7005), jade green (7015) and pine green (7056). Dark copper (7010) and Xmas green (7018) were used for the branch.

Owl

Use pattern 7B (see General Techniques on page 4). The diamond pattern in the church window can best be done as follows. Using a ruler, draw very fine pencil lines in the two diagonal directions and then embroider on top of these. The colours used here are pine green (7056) for the diagonal lines, variegated cranberry/gold/pine green (7027) for the window frame and brass (7005) for the owl. First embroider the diagonal lines of the window followed by the window frame. Use long stem stitch 1-7. Stop at every corner and start again. Embroider the owl using the long stem stitch 1-7 and 1-5 for the short, fine lines. Embroider the details using the standard stem stitch.

Red Robin

This card is ideal for perfectionists, though naturally you are always free to deviate from the instructions. Pierce pattern 7C into the card (see General Techniques on page 4). After piercing the pattern, colour the eye in black.

Pattern 7B

The colours used here are Xmas red (7014) for the breast, variegated black/silver (7023) for the beak, back, wing and feet, silver (7001) for the belly and bottom of the tail, and dark copper (7010) for the ground. Start by embroidering the top of the beak using the long stem stitch 1-3. Lengthen (rather quickly) the stitches to 1-7. The wing is also embroidered from 1 to 7 (1-7). Embroider the belly from the red of the breast to the tail using 1-5. The tail is also done using a

Pattern 7C

length of 1 to 5. Start the red for the breast at the beak using 1-5 and lengthen to 1-7. After the curve, shorten the stitches again so that the line thins out towards the end. Use the standard stem stitch for the feet and 1-5 for the ground.

Peacock

Pierce pattern 7D (page 79) into the card (see General Techniques on page 4). This lovely bird is very easy to embroider. Refer to the coloured picture often when embroidering. The colours used here are variegated jade/purple (7022) and gold (7007). The stitches used are the running stitch for the start of the tail, the long stem stitch from 1 to 5 for the body, the wing, the first two feathers above and the first two feathers below. The other features are embroidered using a stitch from 1 to 7. Embroider stars on the peacock's crown. Also use stars to create the eyes on the tail feathers.

Sympathy Cards

Society is changing, and with it our habits and ways of thinking. Customs surrounding death are characterised these days by a kinder, shared sense of loss. We have learned to deal with death more openly and have made it more discussable. One custom that has not changed is the sending of a sympathy card to surviving relatives. These cards, made with sincerity and care, offer sympathy and comfort in times of loss. You can choose muted colours for the paper and threads, or any colour you feel is appropriate.

Card with Cross

I've chosen a darker coloured paper for this card, though ivory white and other soft hues are also suitable. Pierce pattern 8A or 8B into the card (see General Techniques on page 4). The crosses on both sides are embroidered in gold (7007) and silver (7001) using the loop stitch (see General Techniques on page 7). The blue petals and green leaves of the flower sprigs are embroidered using the loop stitch. The stem of the rose is embroidered using the plait stitch from point 1 on the left to point 3 on the right, and so forth. The rose and green leaf are embroidered using the stem stitch. I have used a variety of different threads for these cards. Finer threads are preferable.

8A

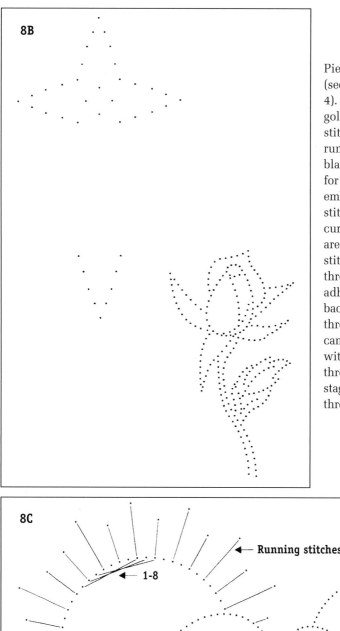

8B

Sun Behind the Clouds

Pierce pattern 8C into the card (see General Techniques on page 4). The sun is embroidered in gold (7007) using the long stem stitch 1-8 and the rays using the running stitch. Variegated black/silver thread (7023) is used for the clouds, which are embroidered using the long stem stitch 1-7 and 1-5 for the short curves. The lines at the bottom are done using very long running stitches and the same variegated threads. After embroidering, adhere pieces of cellotape to the back of the card on top of the threads to prevent tearing. You can also strengthen each thread with a support thread halfway through the stitch. Make sure you stagger the holes for these support threads.

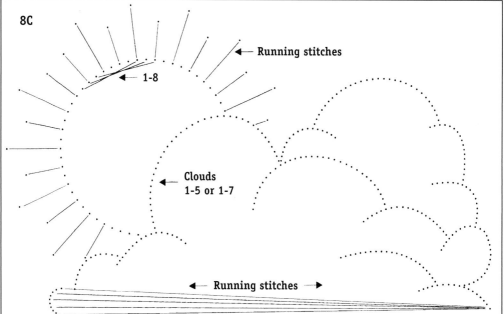

8C

← Running stitches

← 1-8

Clouds
1-5 or 1-7

← Running stitches →

Cross in Ornamental Stitch

Pierce pattern 8D into the card (see General Techniques on page 4). This card can be done quickly and easily. The cross consists of repeatedly embroidered streamers and stars. Choosing the paper and thread colours carefully will ensure a beautifully decorated card. Embroider the cross on a larger card, frame it, and hang it in a special place on the wall. Embroider the streamers in gold (7007) using the long stem stitch from 1 to 5 (1-5). The stars are embroidered in blue (7016) here. Other colour combinations might be more suitable with a different coloured background.

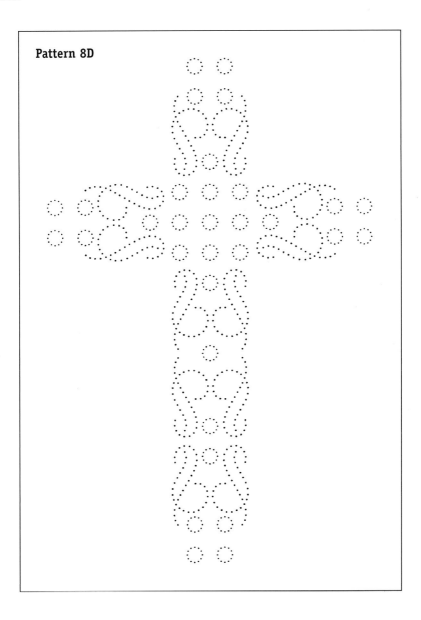

Pattern 8D

Good Wishes

Embroidered cards can be used for a wide variety of occasions. This chapter contains greeting cards that are easy to create. These cards are embroidered in their entirety, though naturally you can choose to embroider only along the edges and glue a photograph, piece of fabric, or 3D picture in the middle. This lets you turn a 'standard' greeting card into a special and unique card that's sure to be remembered.

Happy 2005

Pierce pattern 9A into the card (see General Techniques on page 4). Embroider the curved lines using the long stem stitch 1-5 in gold (7007) and mint (7053). Also do the stars in gold and mint. Embroider the text using the standard stem stitch.

9A

Star

Pierce pattern 9B into the card (see General Techniques on page 4). Embroider the curved lines using the long stem stitch 1-5 in gold (7007), purple (7050) and lavender (7012). The star in the middle is alternately made of embroidered stars in gold, lavender and purple.

Card with Number

Pierce pattern 9C into the card (see General

9B

Techniques on page 4). Embroider the curls using the long stem stitch 1-5 in gold (7007). Embroider the straight lines in the corners and the diamond in lavender (7012). The stars are done here in lavender and purple (7050). The numbers in the middle are embroidered in gold-coloured threads.

Congratulations

Pierce pattern 9D into the card (see General Techniques on page 4). Embroider the curved lines using the long stem stitch 1-5 in purple (7050), gold (7007), and lavender (7012). The diamonds are all done in gold and lavender. Embroider the letter "C" using the long stem stitch 1-5 and the rest of the text using the standard stem stitch and gold-coloured threads.

9C

9D

Christmas Cards

Most cards are sent during the winter holidays. Everyone tries to send a thoughtful, beautiful card and it's always a lovely surprise to receive one. The prettiest cards are given a place of honour on the mantel. Send your loved ones a self-made card and they are sure to proudly display it for everyone to see.

Christmas Tree with Church

Pierce pattern 10A into the card (see General Techniques on page 4). It is especially important to perforate the church precisely. After piercing the pattern, draw a number of support lines (as shown on the pattern). These lines will help you recognise the structure of the tree. Embroider the tree in pine green Sulky thread (7056) and using the filler stitch (see General Techniques on page 7). To make it easier, numbers are given in the pattern. Start with the lowest branch. Embroider from 1 on the bottom right to 1 on the left, from 2 on the left to 2 on the right, from 3 on the right to 3 on the left, and so on, until you reach the end of

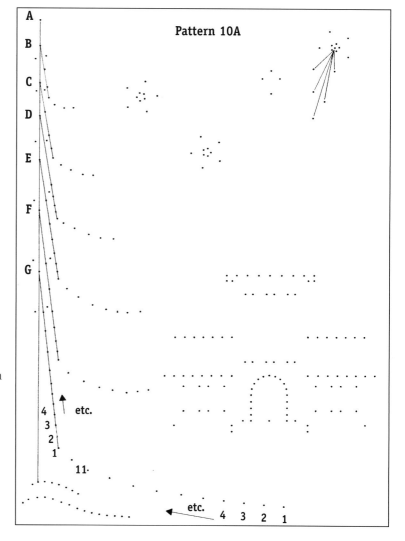

Pattern 10A

34

the two rows of holes. Now embroider the second branch from the bottom using the same method. Continue upwards branch by branch. Every branch has an equal number of holes to the right and left.

From points A through F, embroider two threads downwards at an angle. From G, embroider five threads to the foot of the tree. These five threads form the tree trunk. Finally, embroider a thread on top of every support line you have drawn.

Embroider the rest of the card in gold (7007) and variegated gold/turquoise/pink (7020). Embroider the steeple using the loop stitch. This will ensure that all threads lie neatly alongside each other. The vertical thread of the cross serves as the loop. You should therefore embroider the cross twice and secure it on the back with a piece of cellotape. This will make the loop stronger (see General Techniques on page 7). For the rest of the church, it is helpful to first lightly outline the form on the card. For the narrow windows and rooflines it is especially useful to have the threads on the back run in the same general direction as the threads on the front of the card. This keeps the windows, etc. from becoming deformed.

Candle with Christmas Ball

This card suggests a twisted candle. Pierce pattern 10B into the card (see General Techniques on page 4). Next, make four loops for the four sections of the candle and then make a loop for the flame (see General Techniques on page 7). Embroider the candle and flame using the loop stitch. This will ensure that the threads lie neatly against the card. The arrow shows the location of the first stitch for each section of the candle. The Christmas ball, the holly leaves and berries are embroidered using the long stem stitch 1-5. The halo around the flame is embroidered using running stitches. The colours used here are mint (7053) for the candle, Xmas green (7018) for the holly

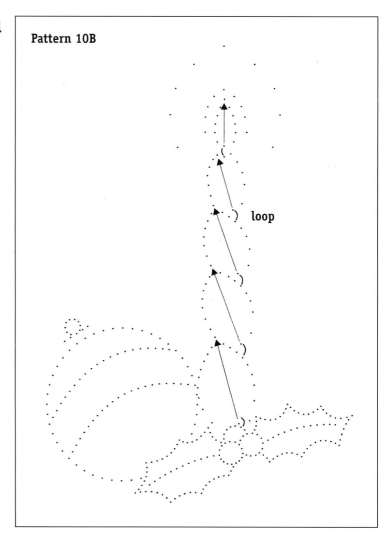

Pattern 10B

loop

leaves, variegated gold/turquoise/pink (7020) for the flame, gold (7007) for the ball and halo around the flame, and Xmas red (7014) for the berries.

Music Stave

Pierce pattern 10C (see General Techniques on page 4). The Treble clef and the stave are embroidered using the long stem stitch 1-5. The standard stem stitch is used for the notes. The stave is embroidered in gold (7007), the Treble clef in mint (7053), and the notes in black (7051). The corners of the card are decorated using a star corner punch. A piece of origami paper is glued under the punched corners.

Reindeer

Pierce pattern 10D (page 79) into the card (see General Techniques on page 4). First, colour in the eyes. The outer edges of the Christmas balls are embroidered using the circle stitch from 1 to 5.

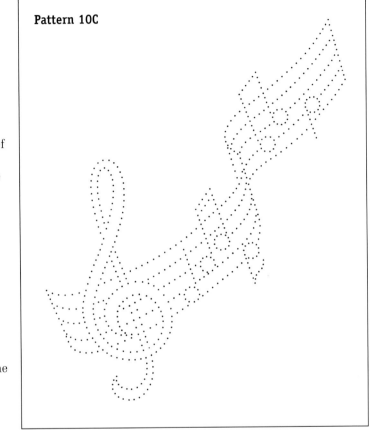

Pattern 10C

The reindeer is embroidered using the long stem stitch 1-7 and 1-5 for the short lines. Stop at each corner and begin again. The colours used here are light copper (7011) for the antlers, dark copper (7010) for the head, pine green (7056), Xmas green (7018) and purple (7050) for the Christmas balls and gold (7007) for the stars.

Whimsical Animals

These cheerful cards are perfect for humorous and joyous occasions. Young and old are sure to appreciate such a card, created just for them. These cards are also ideal for sending a short note instead of writing an entire letter, as there is plenty of space on the inside to write. And because animals appeal to the imagination, you can use these cards for almost any occasion.

Bookworm

Pierce pattern 6A into the card (see General Techniques on page 4). First, colour in the eyes and eyebrows using a gel pen. The colours used here are Xmas green (7018) for the face, body and hands, dark copper (7010) for the glasses, and variegated cranberry/gold/pine green (7027) for the book. Embroider using the long stem stitch 1-5 for the thinner lines and short curves. For the thicker lines, embroider from 1 to 7 (1-7) (see General Techniques on pages 5 and 6).

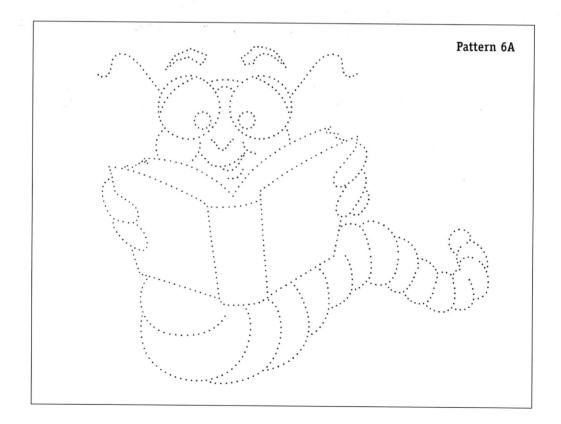

Pattern 6A

Quack

This whimsical duck can be made quickly and easily. Use pattern 6B (see General Techniques on page 4). Colour the eyes in first. Next, embroider the duck in gold (7007) and dark copper (7010). Everything is embroidered using the long stem stitch 1-5 or 1-7.

Frog

Pierce pattern 6C into the card (see General Techniques on page 4). Colour the eyes in first. Next, embroider the spots, starting with the gold-coloured stripes followed by the outline in variegated black/silver (7023) using the standard stem stitch and the long stem stitch 1-5. Embroider the outline of the eyes the same way as the outline of the spots. Embroider the frog itself in Xmas green (7018) using the long stem stitch 1-5 or 1-7. To obtain attractive corners, stop at each corner and start again. Embroider the water lily leaf in pine green (7056) using the long stem stitch 1-9. Do the water lines around the leaf in peacock blue (7052) and blue (7016).

Bunny

Pierce pattern 6D into the card (see General Techniques on page 4). Draw the eye and nose first. The following colours are used here: dark copper (7010) for the bunny, light copper (7011) for the ear, lavender (7012) for the flower, gold (7007) for the stamens, and Xmas green (7018) for the plant. Embroider the flower stem using the plait stitch, filling stitch for the stamens, and the standard stem stitch for the details. Embroider the longer lines using the long stem stitch 1-5 or 1-7.

40

Pattern 6B

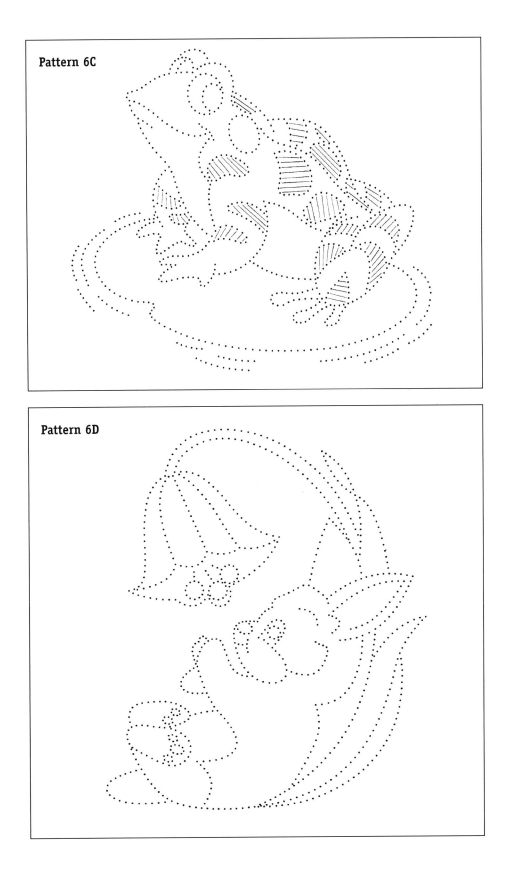

Pattern 6C

Pattern 6D

Early Bloomers

We know winter has come to an end when the snowdrops appear. The magnificent display of colour of the countless crocuses often goes hand in hand with a lovely spring sun and, when the narcissuses start blooming, we know that spring has finally arrived. The golden yellow spring sunflower, with its attractively shaped green leaves, is a perennial that brightens up many a garden on our street every April.

The Snowdrop

The card used here is lilac and round, although this pattern can also be used with a square or rectangular card and different coloured paper. Pierce the border of pattern 16B (page 64) around the edge of a round card and then pierce pattern 11A in the centre of the card. Start with the white colour. A white gel pen works well, as does correction fluid. Embroider the petals and buds using the plait stitch. Start at each point and embroider from 2 to 5 and back again crossways from 5 to 2.

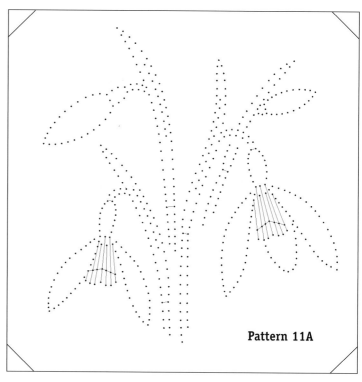

Pattern 11A

Outline using the stem stitch. Embroider the seed buds above the flower using the plait stitch and stem stitch. The skirt of the snowdrop is embroidered using the running stitch. Embroider the green parts using the long stem stitch (1-5), but use the standard stem stitch (1-3) for the curves and thinner lines. The border of the card is done using the stem stitch. The colours used here are silver (7001), Xmas green (7018) and variegated jade/purple (7022) from Sulky.

The Crocus

Use the border of pattern 16B (page 64) for the edges and then pierce pattern 11B in the centre of a round card. The leaves are embroidered in Xmas green (7018) using the plait stitch. The flower is done in purple (7050) using the long stem stitch. You can add one or two short stitches to the start and end of the curves. The stamens are done in gold (7007). If you use a different coloured background, you can embroider the flowers using different coloured threads.

The Narcissus

Pierce pattern 11C into the card. The trumpet of the flower is embroidered in light copper (7011) using the zigzag stitch and stem stitch. For the petals, use gold (7007) and the long stem stitch (1-5). Stop at every corner and start again. Embroider the veins in the petals using the stem stitch (1-3). The leaves and stem in Xmas green (7018) using the stem stitch and the long stem stitch.

The green wavy border is created using the Fiskars 'Victorian' scissors. Decorative edge scissors with small patterns are the most suitable for cutting edges. Make sure you try out the scissors before using them on the card. To cut decorative edging, first draw a number of straight lines, 3 mm apart, on the back of a green card. Hold the card so that the lines are on the left side of the paper and run from bottom to top. Now cut with the scissors against the line to the far left from the bottom to the top. Next, cut

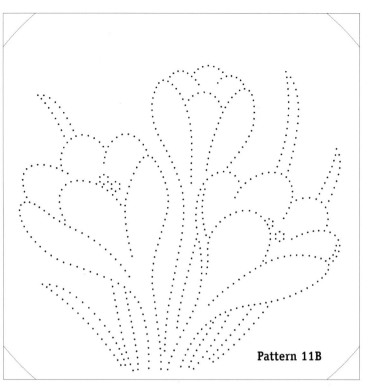

Pattern 11B

Pattern 11C

the second line, and then the third line, and so forth. It may seem odd at first, but this way you can see what you're doing. Place the patterned strips along the edges of the card and secure them with paperclips. Experiment with making corners until you get it right. Place the strips in position on the card. Remove one strip and then glue it onto the card. Repeat with the other strips.

The Spring Sunflower

Pierce pattern 11D into the card. Embroider the heart however you wish, with crisscrossing lines and outlining it using the stem stitch. The colour used here is light copper (7011). Embroider the flower part in gold (7007) and do every stitch twice. Alternately, you could use thicker thread and stitch only once. The stitches of the flowers each form a V, from a single point in the heart and two points on the edge. Start each flower with the reverse V directly above the flower stem. The green is embroidered using the stem stitch (1-3) and the long stem stitch (1-5). You can add a decorative edge using patterned scissors and following the instructions given above for the narcissus.

Four-Leaf Clover (see back cover)

Pierce pattern 11E (page 48) into the card. The four-leaf clover is embroidered in Xmas green (7018). The stem is done using the long stem stitch (1-5). For the leaves, choose a longer stitch, such as from 1 to 7 or 1 to 8. A gold-coloured sequin is sewn in the middle. The curls around the border are done in dark gold (7004) using the long stem stitch (1-5). The pointy shape is done in gold (7007) and Xmas green (7018).

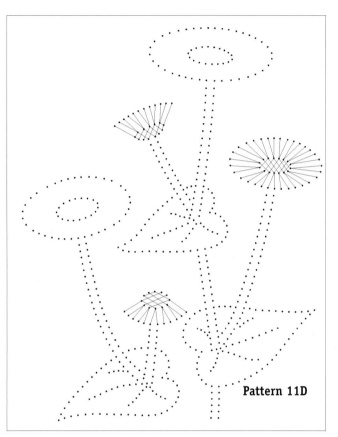

Pattern 11D

New Life

Spring is a source of inspiration year after year. The world around us is full of young green leaves and newborn animals. What better time to create baby cards to have on hand when needed?

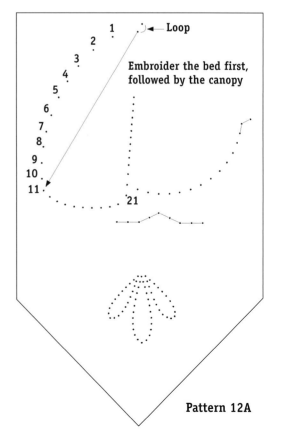

All patterns can be embroidered on standard sized cards. The decorative edges are optional. You can decorate the borders however you wish (see other chapters in this book). Many of these figures are embroidered in gold. It is usually the best colour to choose if the subject matter does not call for a particular colour.

The curl embroidered on the three cards is only shown in pattern 12D with the stork. Take one of the corners of a sturdy card and pierce the pattern into it. Use this corner as a template for piercing the other cards. The patterns in the corners of the cards are embroidered using the stem stitch (standard and long) in variegated light blue/gold/lavender (7024). The best results are obtained if you embroider larger curves with a stitch from 1 to 5 and switch to a stitch from 1 to 3 for the shorter curves.

The borders of the cards are cut out using the 'Imperial' style scissors from Fiskars. The technique used is the same as the one used for the edges of the "Early Bloomers" cards on page 44, except here you should draw the lines 4 mm apart. Once you have cut the line from the bottom to the top, turn over the scissors so that the following line is cut as a mirror image.

Baby Cot

This is a cute card that is quick and easy to create. Pierce pattern 12A into the card. Embroider the bed first in gold (7007). Start with the thread on the bottom left to the upper right. The canopy of the bed is embroidered using the loop stitch (see General Techniques on page 7). Do the (double) loop first and then stitch the first thread from the loop to point 11 and so on.

1 ◦—◀ **Loop**
2
3
4
5
6
7
8
9
10
11

Embroider the bed first, followed by the canopy

21

Pattern 12A

Bear on a Cloud

Resting on a cloud of softness and tenderness - that's our wishes for the newborn baby with this card. Pierce pattern 12B into the card. The cloud is embroidered in peacock blue (7052) using the long stem stitch from 1 to 5 (1-5).

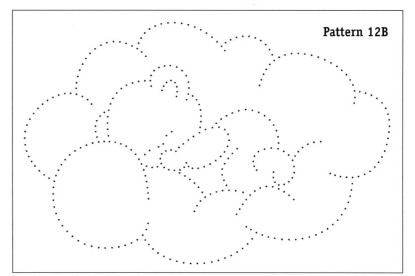

Pattern 12B

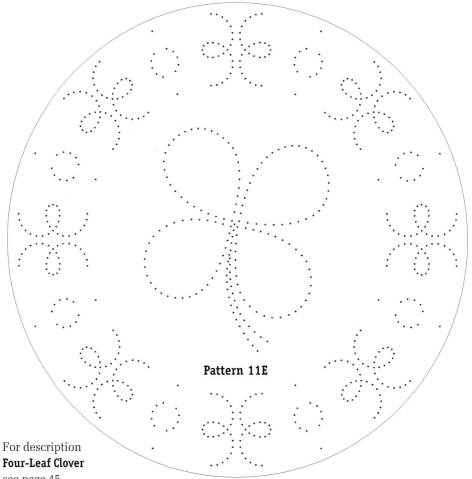

Pattern 11E

For description
Four-Leaf Clover
see page 45.

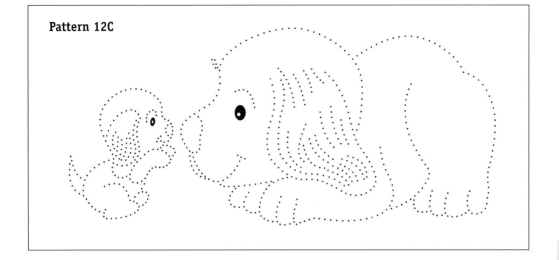

Pattern 12C

Stop at the end of each curve and start again. The bear is shown here in gold (7007). Use the long stem stitch from 1 to 5 and from 1 to 3, and backstitches for the face.

Dog with Puppy

How touching it is when young animals explore their surroundings immediately after birth. Pierce pattern 12C into the card. First colour in the nose and eyes in black, add a small dab of white to the eyes and allow to dry. The dogs are embroidered using the long stem stitch 1-7 for the long, thick lines, 1-5 for the shorter or thinner lines, and the stem stitch 1-3 for the short or thin lines (in the ears of the puppy, for example). The colour used here is gold (7007).

Stork

The stork that brings babies can often be seen in the garden of proud new parents to announce the baby's arrival. Pierce pattern 12D into the card. Use Xmas red (7014) for the stork's beak and feet. Double the stitches for the beak and embroider the legs using the long stem stitch 1-5 and 1-3. Embroider the body in light gold and use the stem stitch 1-5 and 1-3 here as well.

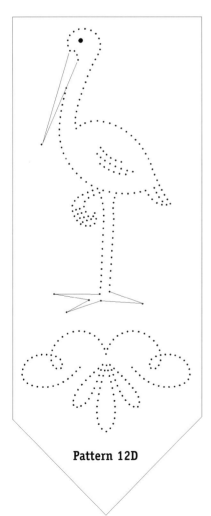

Pattern 12D

Children's Birthday

You wake up on your special day to a house decorated with streamers and balloons, you receive gifts from your friends and family, and you treat everyone to cake. The mailman brings birthday cards from relatives and you proudly display the pretty cards for everyone to see.

Sea Lion with Ball

Pierce the corners of pattern 13D into the card and then pattern 13A between the corners. Colour the nose and eyes in black and the mouth in red. Embroider the sea lion in variegated black/silver (7023) using the long stem stitch 1-3 and 1-5. Stop at every corner and start again. Add two small stitches to the start and end of the embroidered lines to make them equally thick. Embroider the ball in jade green (7015), the contour from 1 to 7 and the lines inside the ball from 1 to 5 and from 1 to 3. The corners are embroidered in jade green and gold (7007).

Kitty

Pierce the corners of pattern 13E (page 53) and then pierce pattern 13B between the corners. Colour in the eyes and nose first using a black gel pen, allow to dry, and then add small dabs of white. The kitty is embroidered here in dark copper (7010). The eyes, mouth and toes are embroidered using the stem stitch, the face using the long stem stitch from 1 to 7, the ears and body from 1 to 5, and so on. Add a few green stitches inside the eyes and do the eyelashes in black. Embroider the ball of yarn in Xmas green (7018) from 1 to 5. The corners are embroidered using the loop stitch in variegated cranberry/gold/pine green (7027).

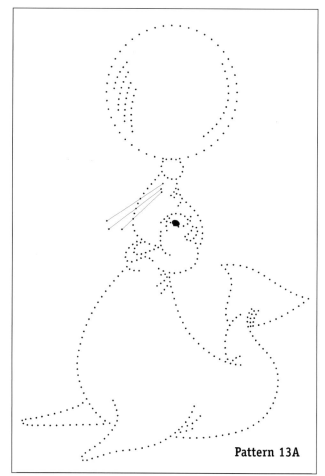

Pattern 13A

Mice

One of the mice is sick and must use a wheelchair until he can walk again. This card is great for sending to children confined to their bed due to illness. Pierce the corners of pattern 13E and then pierce pattern 13C between the corners. Colour in the eyes first. The clothing is embroidered in purple (7050) and rose (7013) using the stem stitch from 1 to 5. With a little imagination, you can embroider the tails using the plait stitch (from 1 to 3). The mice are embroidered in gold (7007) from 1 to 5. The wheelchair is done in Xmas green (7018) and blue (7016). Use variegated gold/turquoise/pink (7020) for the corners and embroider using the loop stitch.

Monkey Faces

These mischievous little monkeys are sure to bring a smile. After piercing pattern 13D, colour in the eyes and noses. Embroider the faces in gold (7007) using the long stem stitch (1-5) and from 1 to 3 or 1 to 4 around the black of the eyes. The hair is done in dark copper (7010) using the stem stitch 1-3 or 1-5. The corners can be embroidered in any colour you want.

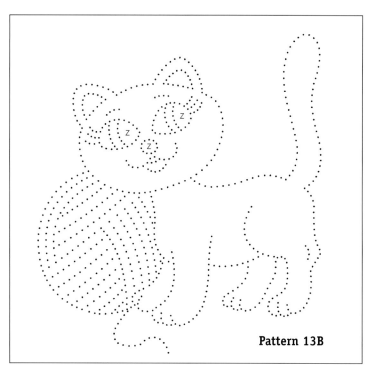

Pattern 13B

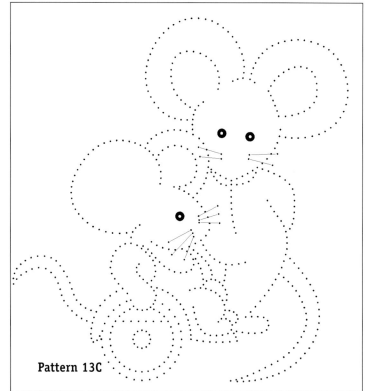

Pattern 13C

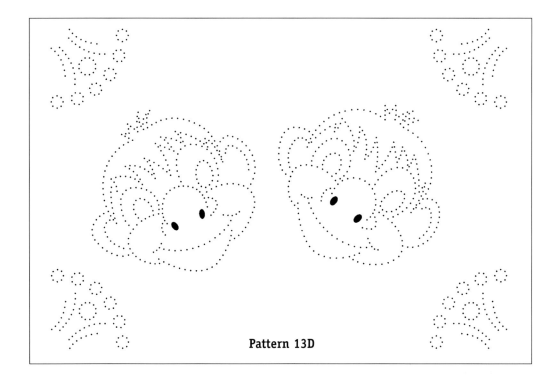

Pattern 13D

Finishing the Cards

The cards shown here with a punched edge or embroidered corners are glued onto an extra large yellow background, though you may finish your cards however you wish.

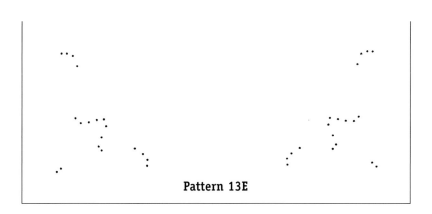

Pattern 13E

Sports All Year Round

Sports can be played any time of year, indoors when the weather outside is uninviting, and outdoors when the good weather beckons. There is a sport for everyone.

Swimming

This swimmer is ready to dive in, but the water appears ready to strike back. Pierce pattern 14C into the card. The colours used here for the swimmer are gold (7007) for the hair, light copper (7011) for the face, arms and legs, variegated cranberry/gold/pine green (7027) for the bikini, silver (7001) for the starting block and blue (7016) for the water. Except for the starting block, the entire card is embroidered using the long stem stitch 1-3, 1-5 and 1-7.

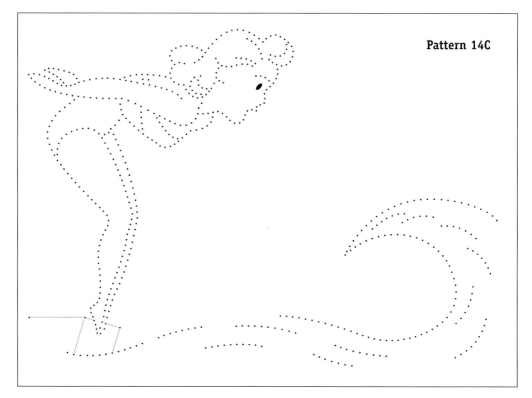

Pattern 14C

Skateboard

A fun card for an athletic young boy, this one is easy to make. Pierce pattern 14A into the card. The colours used here are Xmas green (7018) for the cap, variegated cranberry/gold/pine green

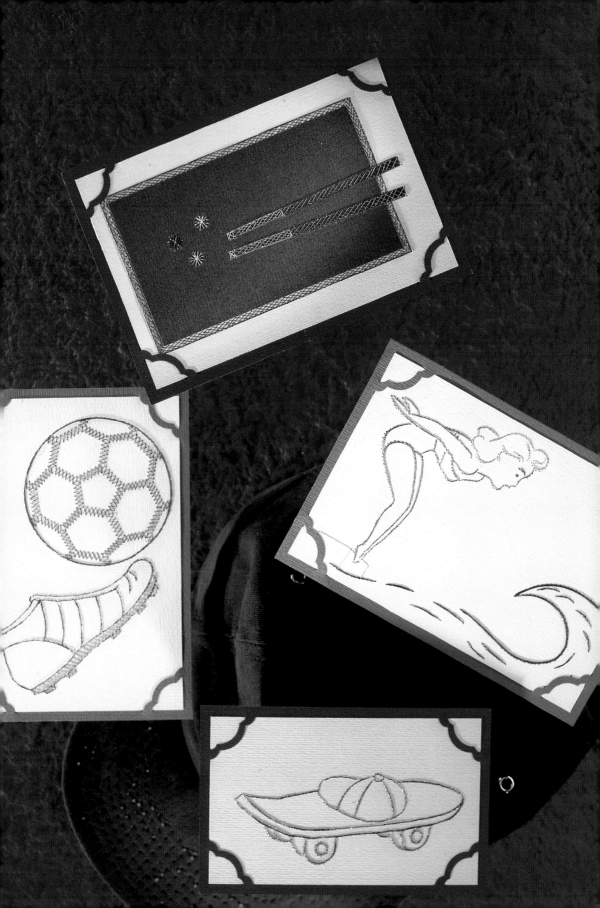

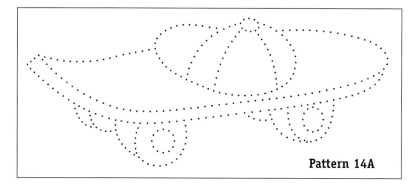

Pattern 14A

(7027) for the board, and purple (7050) for the wheels. Embroider the entire card using the long stem stitch (1-5) and standard stem stitch.

Playing Football

Pierce pattern 14B into the card. Start by embroidering the 20 tripods shown on the pattern. Next, do the cross stitches. Many of the stitches appear lopsided, but that's the way they

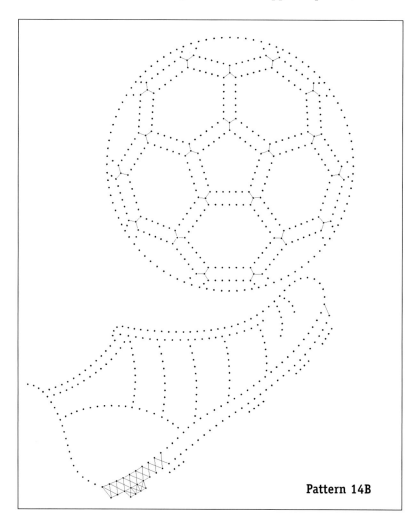

Pattern 14B

should be. Outline the ball using the long stem stitch from 1 to 4 or from 1 to 5. Start the shoe using the cross stitch in the sole and studs. Embroider the rest using the long stem stitch from 1 to 4 and from 1 to 5. Add a small extra stitch to the thin ends of the lines.

Billiards

Place the green card on top of the yellow one and then secure pattern 14D on top of the yellow card using paperclips. Pierce the pattern all the way through, making sure to keep the piercing tool upright. Embroider the outline of the billiard table onto the yellow card from end to end, starting with the short sides. Next, embroider the long sides up to the short sides. Outline the card using the running stitch in lengths of 2 to 3 cm. Now cut the billiard cloth out of the green card. The two billiard cues are cut out along with the cloth! Cut precisely over the middle of the holes. Smear some photo glue along the edges of the cloth and a drop behind the ends of the cues. Glue the cloth to the yellow card, making sure you can still see through the holes for the cues. Embroider the cues and balls. The colours used here are dark copper (7010) for the edge of the table, light copper (7011) for the cues, gold (7007) and silver (7001) for the tips. Do two of the balls in silver and one in copper.

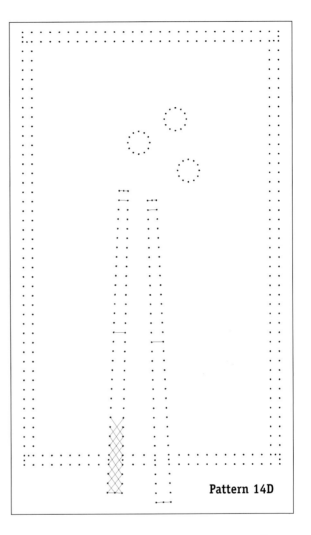

Pattern 14D

Finishing the Cards with a Photo Corner Punch

If you would like a perfect finish, try the following. Draw an arrow pointing towards the top of the card (upper edge of the card) on the background card. Punch the corners of the background card. Place the background card on the embroidered card (top to top). Draw small lines through the openings indicating the maximum width and height of the embroidered card. Cut the edges of the embroidered card, but make sure the lines remain. The cut card should now fit perfectly into the corners (top to top). (Piercing with a needle works better than using a pencil).

A Lovely Summer Day

These cards show the lovely flowers and plants that greet us each summer, letting us enjoy their natural beauty in a variety of shapes and colours.

Upper Right-Hand Card

This cheerful card can be embroidered quickly and easily. Pierce pattern 15C into the card. The stems are embroidered using the long stem stitch. The red flowers and green leaves are done using the filling stitch. The colours used here are Xmas green (7018), pine green (7056) and lavender (7012). Embroider the heart of the large flower, as you desire, using crisscrossing threads. The colour used here is gold (7007). Choose purple (7050) for the edge of the flower and embroider using the long stem stitch from 1 to 4.

Upper Left-Hand Card

After you've pierced the card (pattern 15B), it may look a little odd with such a jumble of holes. To bring some order to the chaos, lightly draw the main lines of the bouquet of wildflowers and continue until the shapes are recognisable. Embroider the ear of wheat in gold (7007). Start at the bottom of the stalk using the long stem stitch from 1 to 7. Gradually switch to a shorter stitch. End with a stitch from 1 to 3. See the section on shortening the long stem stitch on page 5. Embroider the green stalks at the bottom using a stitch from 1-5 and then switch to shorter stitches as you move upwards. Embroider the rest as shown in the drawing.

Pattern 15C

Cornflower and Horseshoe

The flowers can be embroidered two different ways. You can use either the fan stitch or the loop stitch. The fan stitch is shown in pierce pattern 15A for the flower to the far left. This is the easiest stitch to do (see General Techniques on page 4). The loop stitch produces a more attractive result and is therefore preferable (see General Techniques on pages 7 and 8). This stitch is shown for the flower to the far right on the pattern. The two small blue flowers share a single loop, namely, from Point A to Point B. The loop for the blue crown runs from C to D. The uppermost flower has an extra loop from C to E. Embroider approximately half the threads under the C-E loop and the rest under the C-D loop. Embroider the horseshoe in gold (7007) using

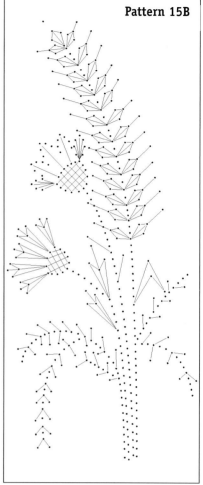

Pattern 15B

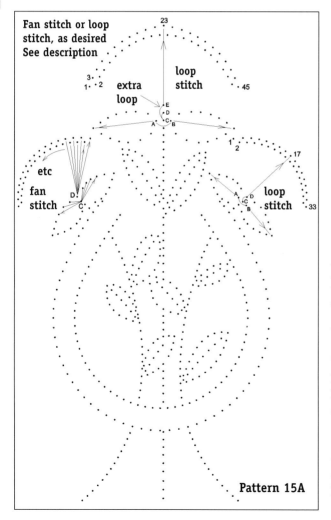

Fan stitch or loop stitch, as desired
See description

loop stitch

extra loop

etc

fan stitch

loop stitch

Pattern 15A

the long stem stitch from 1 to 7. Embroider the greenery in Xmas green (7018) using the long stem stitch from 1 to 5 and 1 to 3 for the veins.

Cat's Tail (Lower Left)

Pierce pattern 15D into the card. Embroider the cat's tail in dark copper (7010) using the plait stitch. Start at the top and embroider from 1 to 7 and then from 7 to 1 on the other side (see General Techniques on page 9 and pattern 15D). Embroider the stalks in Xmas green (7018) using the plait stitch. Start with the stitch from M to 3 on the back and from 3 back to M. Next, stitch from 1 to 4, and so forth (see pattern 15D). The rest of the green parts are embroidered using the long stem stitch.

Finishing the Cards with a Photo Corner Punch

See previous chapter on sports-related cards (page 54). Smooth edges are much easier to work with than serrated edges.

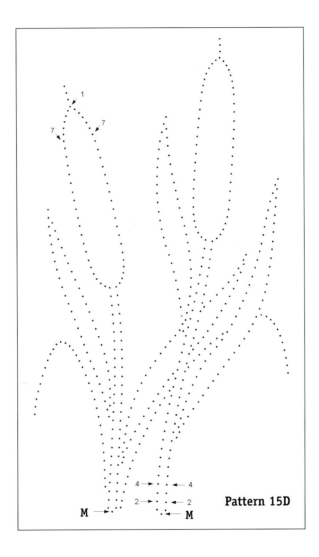

Pattern 15D

A Day Outdoors

There are so many different animals to discover when we venture outdoors. Many of them are difficult to see, though they can often be easily heard. With a little imagination, you can turn these cards into a wonderful celebration of nature.

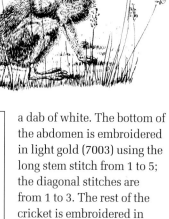

Cricket

We can hear crickets, but we cannot often see them. This shiny little cricket is sitting on a green leaf. After piercing pattern 16A, colour in the eyes black, allow to dry, and add

Pattern 16A

a dab of white. The bottom of the abdomen is embroidered in light gold (7003) using the long stem stitch from 1 to 5; the diagonal stitches are from 1 to 3. The rest of the cricket is embroidered in dark gold (7004) in various stitch lengths. The antennae are done in black (7051). Start with the head with a stitch length of 1-5 and then switch to 1-3 towards the end. Embroider the leaves in Xmas green (7018).

Canaries

These two little birds sharing a branch are as sweet as can be. What could they be talking about? After piercing pattern 16B, colour in the eyes and allow to dry. The branch is embroidered in dark copper (7010) using the long stem stitch 1-5 and 1-3. The canaries are done in gold (7007). For the larger lines in the body, use the long stem stitch from 1 to 7, and then 1-5 and 1-3 for the rest. The beaks are done here in mint (7053) and lavender (7012). The border is embroidered in silver/rose/jade (7029) using a stitch from 1 to 4. The cream-coloured card is 126 mm in diameter and the green card is 132 mm in diameter. If you glue a piece of thread between the two, you can hang the card.

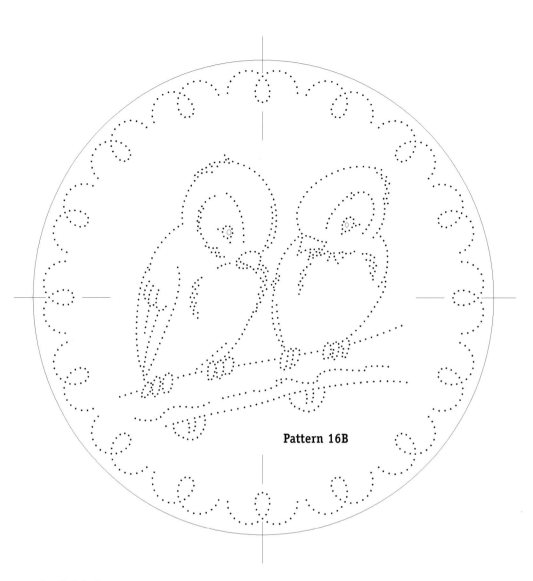

Pattern 16B

Ladybird

I thought this ladybird was just so adorable that I had to embroider him for you. After piercing pattern 16C, colour the eyes in black and then add a dab of white. I've used a pencil to make the white slightly grey. The eyes are embroidered directly around the coloured-in parts. Embroider the spots on the back with crisscrossing black (7051) threads and outline them using the stem stitch. The head, arms and feet are also embroidered in black using the stem stitch. The shell is embroidered in Xmas red (7014) using a stitch from 1 to 5. In the heart of the flower, embroider crisscrossing lines in dark copper (7010) and outline with a stitch from 1 to 4. Embroider the edge of the flower in gold (7007). The flower stem is done in jade green (7018) using the plait stitch.

Deer

After piercing pattern 16D, colour in the eyes, nose and spots in black and allow to dry. Embroider the deer in gold (7007) using the long stem stitch 1-5 and 1-3. Embroider around the eye, nose, etc. in dark copper (7010) using the stem stitch 1-3. Embroider the grass and leaves in

Pattern 16C

Xmas green (7018). Double the stitches for the grass. The tree is done in dark copper (7010) using the plait stitch. Embroider the bird in mint (7053) using the stem stitch 1-5 and 1-3.

Pattern 16D

Autumn is Upon us Once Again

The start of autumn always has its charm. The sun appears a little lower in the sky, the days are cooler, and the evenings mild. The woods still enjoy the afterglow of summer and the animals have an abundance of food. The mushrooms start appearing in all shapes and sizes, and the leaves on the trees start to change gradually into magnificent colours.

Leaves have been punched into the corners of the cards shown here. If you have any of the background card remaining, it is much easier to simply punch the leaves out of this paper and glue them to the embroidered card.

Hat

A hat can be elegant, fashionable, or just plain fun. The larger models protect you against the hot rays of the sun and any unexpected rain showers. Pierce pattern 17A into the card. The

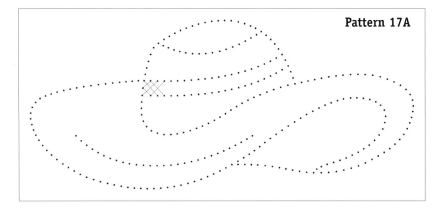

Pattern 17A

hatband is embroidered using the plait stitch in gold (7007) (see drawing). The rest of the hat is embroidered in light copper (7011) using the long stem stitch from 1 to 7. This creates thick lines and wide curves. The feather is a gift from our Australian finches.

Mushrooms

After piercing pattern 17C, the mushrooms can be coloured in using a lilac pastel coloured pencil and then rubbed using a cotton bud. The card is embroidered using various lengths of stem stitches. For the head of the mushroom, use variegated jade/purple (7022), variegated black/silver (7023) for the stems, and pine green (7056) for the oak leaf. Green has been chosen here because of the background colour. The snail shell is embroidered in variegated

Pattern 17C

cranberry/gold/pine green (7027) and the snail itself in black (7051). The tips of the black feelers at the top of the head are made using a gel pen.

Deer

This deer, in all its grace and dignity, is resting yet still keeping an eye on his surroundings because, after all, rest is a relative notion in the animal world. After piercing pattern 17D, colour in the eyes, nose and hooves using a black gel pen. Allow to dry. Add a dab of white to the eye. Embroider the spots on the back and the antlers in dark copper (7010) using the long stem stitch from 1-3 and 1-5. For the spots on the black, see the section on the filling stitch on page 7 under General Techniques. The rest of the deer is embroidered in gold (7007) using stitch lengths of 1-5 and 1-3.

Cloud

This cloud appears to enjoy blowing the coloured leaves off the trees and then playing with them a little while. Pierce pattern 17B into the card. The threads used here are no longer available, but the variegated gold/turquoise/ pink (7020) from Sulky also works well. Do the long straight running stitches originating from the mouth first. Do each stitch twice. The rest of the embroidery work will secure these long threads. Use the long stem stitch in varying lengths, i.e. from 1 to 7 for the thick curves, from 1 to 5 for the somewhat thinner lines, and from 1 to 3 and backstitches for the small lines. The small colourful leaves are punched out of different coloured paper.

Pattern 17D

Pattern 17B

Autumn Comfort

As the weather turns colder at the end of autumn, we often retreat indoors to enjoy a cosy fire, eat and drink with friends, and pass the time with special hobbies, giving this time of year its own special charm.

The cards in this chapter are cut out using a serration tool and then glued to a different coloured background. The corners are decorated with embossing. This gives the cards a more elegant look, though they are equally attractive without the added decoration.

Coffee Corner

Pierce pattern 18A into the card. The flowers on the pot and cup are embroidered in blue (7016). The rest of the card is done in peacock blue (7052). Embroider the small lines using the stem stitch and the longer lines using the long stem stitch. The edge of the table is embroidered using the plait stitch. Outline the plait stitch with running stitches approx. 2 cm long.

Pattern 18A

Cards

Pierce pattern 18B into the card. This card is embroidered almost entirely using the long stem stitch 1-5 and 1-3. Only the clubs symbol is embroidered using the filling stitch. The colours used here are blue (7016) for the sleeve, light copper (7011) for the hand, and red (7054) and black (7051) for the cards.

The Rocking Chair

Cats seem to visibly enjoy a warm spot in the sun or a place to laze away the day. A little bit of attention is all they need to purr with pleasure. Pierce pattern 18C into the card. The chair is embroidered in dark copper (7010) and the cat with variegated black/silver (7023). Use the long

Pattern 18B

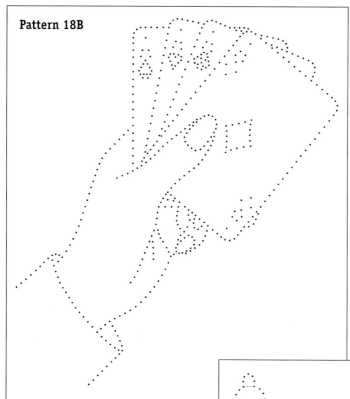

stem stitch 1-5 for the long lines and 1-3 for the short lines and curves. Embroider the thin bars of the chair using cross stitches and outline them with the running stitch.

Wine Cooler

Pierce pattern 18D (page 80) into the card. The top of the bottle is embroidered in gold (7007) using the zigzag stitch and the neck using the plait stitch. Both are outlined using the stem stitch. Embroider the rest of the bottle in pine green (7056) using the long stem stitch 1-5. Do the bucket in light copper (7011). To

produce attractive cross stitches, it is advisable to start in the middle of the front and then to embroider to the left and right. It is more difficult to start on the left or right side because these stitches are lopsided. Embroider the rest of the bucket using the long stem stitch. Add one or two small stitches to the thin ends of the lines. Embroider the water rings in variegated cranberry/gold/pine green (7027) using the long stem stitch 1-5, and the semicircle using the stem stitch 1-3.

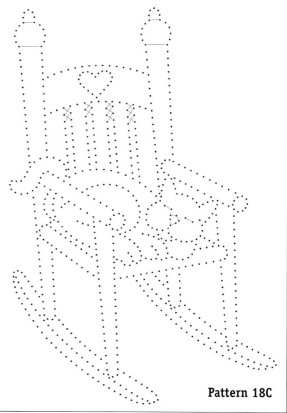

Pattern 18C

Lovely Christmas and New Year's Greetings

This chapter includes two Christmas and two New Year's cards, including the beautiful wall lantern shown on the cover of the book. You could embroider this card for yourself or as a greeting card, wishing someone a bright New Year.

Pattern 19A

Wall Lantern

Take your time to make this card a true ornamental piece. Pattern 19A fits on a standard, round or square card. Cross stitches are embroidered between the straight lines of the lantern and the wall plate in black (7051). They are outlined with long running stitches in gold. Use the filling stitch for the ball under the lamp. Embroider the curls and curves using the long stem stitch 1-5 and 1-3 in dark gold (7004). For the candle, use the backstitch and stem stitch and any colours you desire. A gold-coloured background card gives the lantern an aristocratic touch.

Church

Pierce the border of pattern 16B (page 64) and then pierce pattern 19B into the centre of the card. Mint (7053) was chosen here for the ground and was embroidered using a stitch length of 1 to 4. The thin ends of the curves can be left thin. The rest of the card is embroidered in gold (7007). Embroider the border using the long stem stitch from 1 to 5. The backstitch and stem stitch are used for the doors and windows of the church. Do the rest using long running stitches, as shown in the drawing.

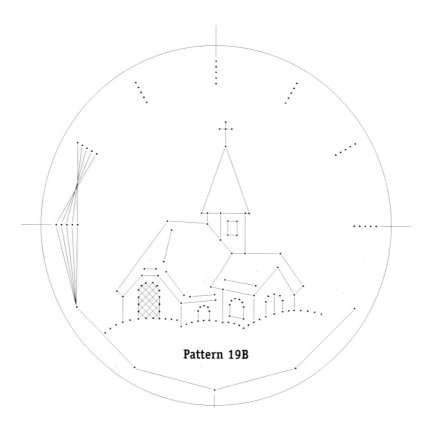

Pattern 19B

Five Candles

If you plan to make several copies of this card, it is a good idea to first make a perforation template of pattern 19C (page 80). Fasten the template or pattern to a corner of a square card and pierce the curl all the way through. Do this three times. When piercing the fourth corner, pierce the candles as well. This sequence helps you avoid mistakes. Embroider the candles using the plait stitch and the flames using the loop stitch. Outline the bottom of the candles. Embroider the figures in the corners using the long stem stitch 1-3 and 1-5. The color is gold (7007).

Clock Dial Card

Some dial cards have a square shape and some have a round one. The round one is less heavy and therefore less expensive to send. If you are unable to buy a dial card, you can always make one yourself. The inner card is a complete circle with a 12.5 cm diameter and the outer card is around 13.5 cm in diameter. The clock is embroidered on the front of the dial card. Secure the bottom part of pattern 19D to the front of the dial card. Line up the circle in the pattern with the

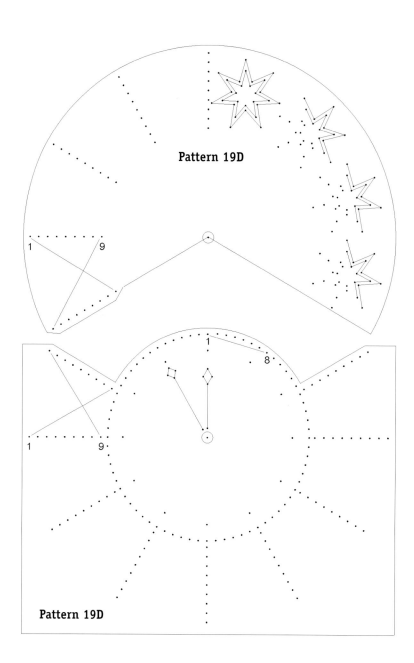

Pattern 19D

Pattern 19D

hole in the card. Fold the card open and pierce the pattern through it. Embroider the small hour markers of the clock using double stitches. Embroider the circle using a stitch from 1 to 8. Embroider the border around the clock as shown in the drawing. The colour used here is gold (7007).

Secure the upper part of pattern 19D to the round dial, also lining up the circle in the pattern with the hole in the card. Pierce the pattern into the two sections of the dial. You can even use a sticker for the third segment of the dial, write a note, or pierce stars or any other pattern. Embroider the dial as shown in the drawing.

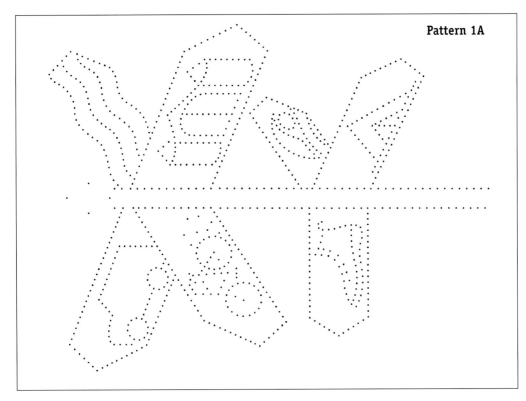

Pattern 1A

For description **Signpost** see page 10.

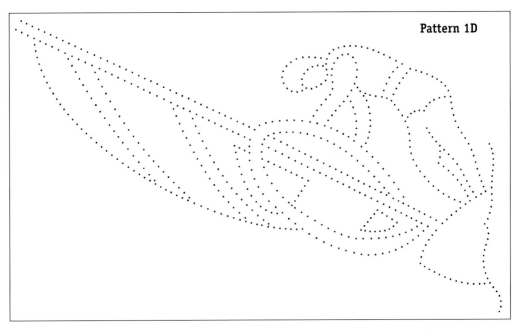

Pattern 1D

For description **Surfer** see page 13.

Pattern 5A

For description **Madonna** see page 18.

Pattern 7D

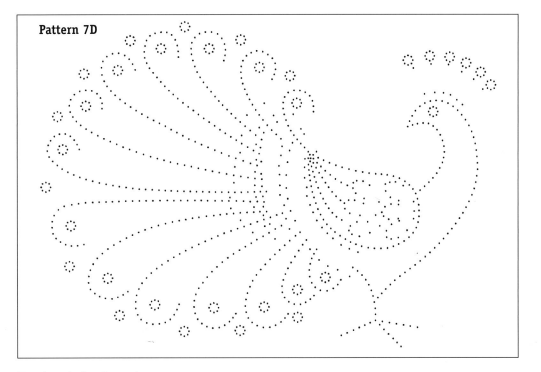

For description **Peacock** see page 25.

Pattern 10D

For description **Reindeer** see page 37.

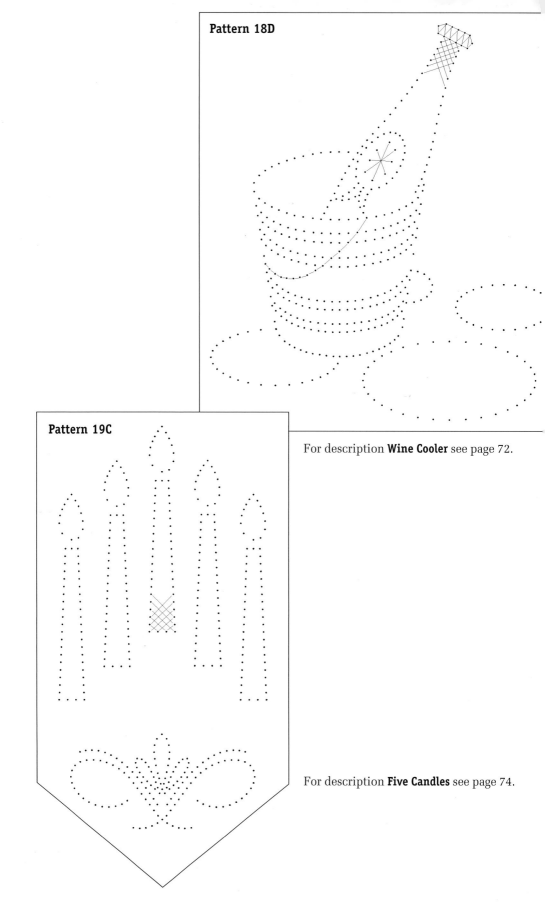

Pattern 18D

For description **Wine Cooler** see page 72.

Pattern 19C

For description **Five Candles** see page 74.